**Antonia Barber** was born into a theatrical family and studied at University College, London. Her first children's novel, *The Ghosts*, was runner-up for the Carnegie medal and was later filmed as *The Amazing Mr Blunden*. Her first book for Frances Lincoln was *Tales from Grimm* and was selected as one of Child Education's Best Books. Her most recent book for Frances Lincoln is *Hidden Tales from Eastern Europe*. Antonia divides her time between a converted oast house in Kent and a harbourside cottage in Cornwall.

**Meilo So** was brought up in Hong Kong and studied art in Oxford and Brighton. She is a part-time lecturer and a freelance illustrator. Her other book for Frances Lincoln is *Wishbones*, retold by Barbara Ker Wilson. It was chosen as one of the Children's Books of the Year in 1994. Meilo lives and works in Hong Kong.

For Peter and Jemma – A.B.

For my niece Tung Hei (Winter Morning Sun) – M.S.

First published in Great Britain in 1995 by
Frances Lincoln Children's Books, 4 Torriano Mews,
Torriano Avenue, London NW5 2RZ
www.franceslincoln.com

First paperback edition 1996

British Library Cataloguing in Publication Data available on request

ISBN 978-0-7112-1085-1

Set in Bembo

Printed in China

9 8 7 6 5

# THE
# MONKEY
# AND THE
# PANDA

ANTONIA BARBER

Illustrated by MEILO SO

**F**

FRANCES LINCOLN
CHILDREN'S BOOKS

Long, long ago, to the east of the sunrise, there once lived a Monkey and a Panda. The Monkey was lean and lithe and lively. The Panda was fat and furry and friendly.

The children of the village loved them both. When they played, they loved the Monkey, who was noisy and naughty and made them laugh. When they grew tired, they went seeking the Panda, who was quiet and comfortable and soft to sleep upon.

But the Monkey grew jealous of the Panda, for he thought the children loved her more.

Each day his tricks grew wilder as he tried to keep the children laughing. His antics caused havoc in the village, until the villagers longed to be rid of him. But they were gentle people and did not wish to harm him.

Close by the village lay a ruined temple. The monks had gone away into a far land, all but one wise old man who was too frail to cross the high mountains. The people of the village brought him food and cared for his needs, and in return he gave them his wisdom.

When they told him of the Monkey's terrible tricks,
the old man smiled.

"Master," they said, "it is no laughing matter!"

"No, indeed!" said the old man, straightening his face.
"I see that you have a real problem. Bring the Monkey
to me and I will talk to him."

The people came, bringing the Monkey, who was cross and sulking.

"Set him down," said the old man gently, "and leave us alone together." Then he asked the Monkey why he had grown so troublesome.

"It is all the Panda's fault," said the Monkey.

"How can that be?" asked the old man, "for the Panda eats and sleeps in the bamboo grove and harms no-one."

"What you say is true," said the Monkey, "and yet the children love her. However hard I try to make them laugh, sooner or later they go to her. Yet judge between us, Master, if I am not better in every way!"

The old man thought for a while. Then he said:

"Is it a judgement you seek? Would you have one better and the other worse? If so, we must see what the Panda has to say for herself."

He lifted the Monkey on to his shoulder and set off to the bamboo grove. And the children, who were hiding among the ruins, stole after them.

They found the Panda sitting in the middle of the grove, eating bamboo shoots.

The old man greeted her and she nodded in return. But she did not speak, for she had good manners and her mouth was full.

"You see," said the Monkey, "she has nothing to say for herself."

"Panda, my friend," said the old man, "I have come to judge between you and the Monkey, which is worthier."

The Panda went on chewing peacefully, and if she was surprised by their mission, she did not show it.

"Each shall speak in turn," said the old man, settling himself upon the ground. And the children hid among the tall stems of the bamboo grove to see what would happen.

The Monkey could not wait to begin.

"I am better than Panda," he boasted, "because there is nowhere that is not mine. From the tallest tree-top to the forest floor, all is my kingdom. I can climb, I can swing, I can leap, I can fly - well, almost. But as for the Panda, she just sits in the bamboo grove all day long and never goes anywhere."

The Panda said nothing. She listened to the rustle of the leaves all about her. She watched the pale sunlight as it broke through the mist. It seemed to her that the bamboo grove was the loveliest place in all the world.

"I am more cunning than the Panda," the Monkey went on. "I find fruit in the treetops, take eggs from the birds' nests, smell honey in the hollow tree. I am even cleverer than the villagers, for sometimes I steal their food."

The Panda said nothing, for her mouth was full of young, green leaves. They were fresh and crisp and sweet on her tongue. It seemed to her that the bamboo shoots had the most delicious taste in all the world.

"You must admit that I am more fun than the Panda,"
said the Monkey. "My tricks make the children laugh, my
daring makes them gasp. I am bolder and braver and a great
deal livelier. Compared to me, the Panda is just boring."

Still the Panda said nothing – for she had fallen asleep.
She dreamed of the sunlight and the green leaves quivering
in the wind and the taste of the bamboo shoots on her
tongue. And it seemed to her that her dream was the best
dream in all the world.

Now the Monkey grew desperate, and his boasting grew ever more fantastic.

"I can ride on the clouds," he cried. "I can speed with the wind. I can travel over the mountains to the world's end. Why, I have fought with dragons and rescued princesses!"

When they heard this, the children stole out of the bamboo grove and gathered silently around him.

Then the Monkey told them a long tale of magic and monsters, of his brave deeds and bold rescues. As he talked, he held the children enthralled and watched their dark eyes grow wide with wonder.

But if you ask me "Was it true?" I can only tell you that all
these things had happened in the Monkey's dreams, and that in
his dreams they *were* true.

As the children listened, they remembered their own dreams,
which they had forgotten upon waking; and the Monkey gave
their dreams back to them.

When the Monkey's story was ended, the children clamoured
for more.

But the old man hushed them, and turning to the Panda,
said, "Panda, you too must speak, if I am to judge between you
and the Monkey."

Then the Panda woke with her dream still about her, and
out of her love for the bamboo grove, which was her home and
her life, she spoke at last. Her voice was as soft as the wind
stirring the leaves, and she said:

"Whisper in the wind, shelter in the storm,
Catching the sun's gleam in the mist of dawn.
Crisp in my mouth, sweet on my tongue,
You become me, we become one."

And the children, who had played all their lives in the
bamboo grove and had never really noticed it, looked up
at the moving leaves outlined against the sunlight and
saw them truly for the first time.

The old man watched and smiled, and he said, "How rich our lives have become! Monkey has taken us to the ends of the world and Panda has shown us into the heart of it. Who am I to judge between them?

Cherish the Monkey, my children, for he is a very great Storyteller, and honour the Panda, for she is a Poet."

# MORE TITLES FROM
# FRANCES LINCOLN CHILDREN'S BOOKS

## HIDDEN TALES FROM EASTERN EUROPE
### Antonia Barber
### Illustrated by Paul Hess

Over the past few years the walls of Eastern Europe have crumbled
to reveal a rich variety of peoples and cultures. Here is a celebration
of some of the stories from Russia, Slovenia, Poland, Slovakia,
Croatia, Serbia and Romania.

ISBN 978-0-7112-2118-5

## TALES FROM GRIMM
### Antonia Barber
### Illustrated by Margaret Chamberlain

This sparkling collection of folktales from the Brothers Grimm
is peopled by characters as real as you and me. Universal favourites such as
*Snow White* and *Hansel and Gretel* are included along with several exciting,
lesser-known tales – all splendidly retold by Antonia Barber.

ISBN 978-0-7112-1341-8

## WISHBONES
### Barbara Ker Wilson
### Illustrated by Meilo So

Wishbones, magic fishbones that make every dream come true…
From south of the clouds comes this oriental fable, weaving riches
and sorrows into the enchanted tale of a golden-eyed fish, a lost slipper
and a king's search for his bride.

ISBN 978-0-7112-1415-6

Frances Lincoln titles are available from all good bookshops.
You can also buy books and find out more about your favourite titles,
authors and illustrators on our website: www.franceslincoln.com